IMAGES
of America

CARLISLE

On the Cover: West High Street is pictured in the late 1800s with a Cumberland Valley Railroad train coming down the street among the horses and buggies. (Courtesy of Cumberland County Historical Society.)

IMAGES
of America

CARLISLE

Beverly J. Bone

ARCADIA
PUBLISHING

ISBN 978-1-4671-0510-1

Published by Arcadia Publishing
Charleston, South Carolina

Printed in the United States of America

Library of Congress Control Number: 2020931401

For all general information, please contact Arcadia Publishing:
Telephone 843-853-2070
Fax 843-853-0044
E-mail sales@arcadiapublishing.com
For customer service and orders:
Toll-Free 1-888-313-2665

Visit us on the Internet at www.arcadiapublishing.com

To Sarah and Deborah, who encourage and support my historical pursuits.

Contents

Acknowledgments		6
Introduction		7
1.	Churches	9
2.	Community Organizations	25
3.	Downtown Businesses	45
4.	Residential Homes	91
5.	Hotels and Taverns	101
6.	Transportation	117
7.	Significant Events	121
About the Cumberland County Historical Society		127

ACKNOWLEDGMENTS

I would like to thank the Cumberland County Historical Society (CCHS) for giving me the opportunity to write this book. I particularly want to acknowledge all the help and support provided by Richard Tritt, photography curator at CCHS, and his assistant, Robert Schwartz. I would also like to express appreciation for the assistance provided by Cara Curtis, librarian of CCHS, and David Smith, a member of the CCHS board of directors. Special thanks to my daughters, Sarah and Deborah Bone, for all the support they have given me.

All photographs are courtesy of the Cumberland County Historical Society.

Introduction

Carlisle, Pennsylvania, is the county seat of Cumberland County, which was formed in 1750. At that time, the Cumberland County boundaries extended from the Susquehanna River to as far as Pittsburgh. Cumberland County is frequently known as "Mother Cumberland" since 48 counties were created from its original boundaries. Carlisle was planned and founded in 1751. It was named after the town of Carlisle in England. Carlisle was incorporated as a borough in 1782. Its original plan was a square plot of land bounded by the present-day North, East, South, and West Streets, encompassing four blocks in each direction. This book will focus on this core section of Carlisle.

The town square was planned as the center of civic and judicial life. It had a courthouse, an Anglican church, and a market house on three of the corners. In 1766, a Presbyterian church was located on the fourth corner of the square.

During the French and Indian War, Carlisle was the westernmost encampment for British soldiers. During the Indian conflicts, the western settlers would fall back to Carlisle for safety. After the Indian uprisings were somewhat settled, Carlisle became the gateway for westward movement and a trading center for goods going to the eastern markets.

Carlisle prospered during the Revolutionary War by serving as an armory and supply center. It was the home of many patriots, including James Wilson and James Smith, signers of the Declaration of Independence. It was also the home of Molly Pitcher, heroine of the Battle of Monmouth, New Jersey. In 1794, Pres. George Washington and Secretary of the Treasury Alexander Hamilton traveled to Carlisle on their journey to put down the Whiskey Rebellion.

Carlisle became known as an educational center with the founding of Dickinson College in 1783. The college granted the first law degree in Pennsylvania in 1836. In that same year, Carlisle became the first area in Pennsylvania to provide a high school for public education. Today, Carlisle is the home of the United States Army War College, Dickinson College, and the Penn State Dickinson School of Law.

The town expanded with the establishment of the Cumberland Valley Railroad in 1837. Carlisle is in the middle of Cumberland Valley's heartland and thus is the center for agricultural markets as well as industrial enterprises. Both of these markets blossomed further with the arrival of the railroad. The railroad was so important to Carlisle that the main line was placed in the center of one of its two main streets. The trains traveled down the center of High Street, and the tracks were elevated in some sections until 1936. Carlisle is only 18 miles west of Harrisburg, the state capital of Pennsylvania; the railroad made it easier to travel to the capital and to points farther east to sell products.

In June 1863, the Confederate army attacked and occupied the town in the days before the Battle of Gettysburg. There are still scars on some of the buildings from the skirmishes that occurred in the downtown streets. East Street was the skirmish line between the Union and Confederate troops. Carlisle was saved from further damage because the Confederate troops were ordered to march toward Gettysburg.

After the Civil War, many changes took place in Carlisle. In 1879, Brig. Gen. Richard Pratt formed the Carlisle Indian Industrial School on the grounds of the Carlisle Barracks. The purpose of the school was to force the Native American youths to assimilate to Euro-American culture. One of its students, Jim Thorpe, became known worldwide as an outstanding Olympic athlete. During the late 1800s, Carlisle continued to thrive with the establishment of more industries, such as the Frog Switch Manufacturing Company, which made railroad switches, and other factories that made shoes, clothing, and a variety of products for the railroad and homes.

In the 20th century, industry continued to expand with the establishment of the Carlisle Tire and Rubber Company, C.H. Masland Company, and the quartz crystal industry. With the creation of the Pennsylvania Turnpike and the establishment of interstate highways, Carlisle became the "Trucking Capitol of the World." Today, Carlisle is strategically located with access to two major highways and the Pennsylvania Turnpike. Carlisle is now a huge distribution center for numerous products shipped nationwide.

Carlisle has not forgotten its vast and changing history. In 1976, the National Register of Historic Places designated the Carlisle Historic District, covering 36 square blocks. In 2004, First Lady Laura Bush designated Carlisle a Preserve America Community, the second city in Pennsylvania to receive this designation. It has preserved its history through its buildings, its stories, and its community. Carlisle continues to honor its past while moving forward with its preservation programs, its celebrations of bygone times, and its community spirit.

One

Churches

The First Presbyterian Church congregation was formed in 1734. The church acquired land from William Penn's heirs on the northwest corner of the square in 1766. The construction of the two-story building designed by architect Robert Carter was completed in 1772. Carlisle patriots met here to select delegates for the Continental Congress. This delegation included James Wilson, James Smith, and George Ross, signers of the Declaration of Independence.

Before the building of the church on the square, the First Presbyterian congregation worshipped in a log structure at Meeting House Springs, approximately two miles west of Carlisle. Although this structure is no longer present, the congregation's old graveyard still exists at this location, as seen here. The oldest grave in the cemetery, dated 1744, was for Jane Thomson. She was the wife of the first pastor, Samuel Thomson.

This is a view of the interior of the church on the 150th anniversary of the signing of the Declaration of Independence in 1926. Another historical event involving the church occurred on October 5, 1794, when Pres. George Washington and Secretary of the Treasury Alexander Hamilton worshipped here on their way to quell the Whiskey Rebellion in western Pennsylvania.

Many renovations and additions to the First Presbyterian Church have occurred through the years. In 1872, a tower was added, and in 1951, a new one-story annex wing was built. The annex includes a fellowship hall, Sunday school rooms, a parlor, and a minister's office. In keeping with the original stone structure, the annex was built of limestone. This photograph shows the annex, tower, and original meetinghouse structures.

Emory Methodist Episcopal Church was built in 1858 at the northeast corner of West and Pomfret Streets. The church was owned by Dickinson College. The brick structure represented the Victorian Gothic style of architecture. From 1863, the building was used as a women's college, a grammar school, and by the Dickinson Law School. In 1919, the United Brethren Church bought the property, and it was later razed.

In 1779, a title for a land parcel was deeded to the Catholic Church, and in 1784, a log structure was built at 140 East Pomfret Street. St. Patrick Church was the first Catholic congregation in the United States to be named after Ireland's patron saint. The first brick structure was built in 1806 and enlarged in 1823. This church was destroyed by fire in 1858, and a larger church was erected and dedicated in 1859. The photograph above shows the third church built on the site. In 1891, an expansion was built to include a convent and school known as St. Katharine Hall. The sisters taught Carlisle children and children from the Carlisle Indian School. The photograph below shows, from left to right, the rectory, the church, and St. Katharine Hall.

The First Evangelical Lutheran Church was chartered in 1765. The first church structure was built in 1810 at 44 North Bedford Street at a cost of $316.30. In 1851, this church was destroyed by fire. During the reconstruction, the congregation held its services at the Second Presbyterian Church. In 1898, Pastor Henry Wiles designed plans for a new church. The building seen at right at the southeast corner of South Bedford and East High Streets was dedicated in 1901 with its 135-foot Italian Renaissance tower. The photograph below shows the interior of the church. In 1966, a new wing was added. Today, the tower of the First Evangelical Lutheran Church continues to be a Carlisle landmark and beacon to the community.

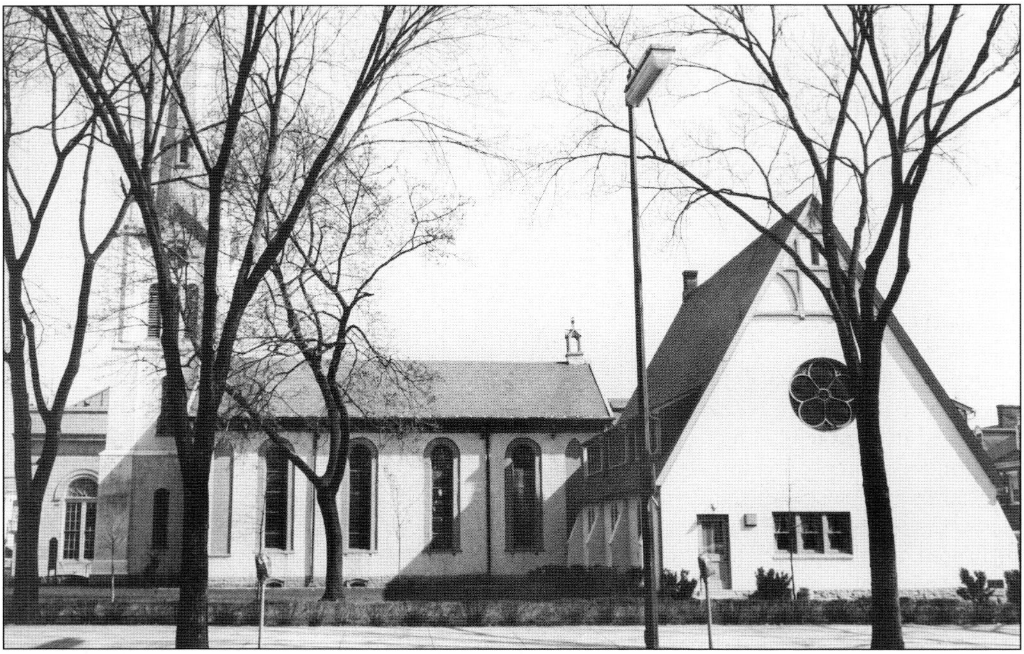

St. John Episcopal Church is located at 1 North Hanover Street on land reserved in the 1750s by the William Penn family for use by the Church of England. The first building was a rustic log structure constructed in the 1750s, which also served as the county courthouse. A small stone church was built in the 1760s. The current building, seen above, was erected in 1826 using stone from the previous structure. The photograph below is an interior view of the sanctuary showing the nave, altar, and pews. Members of Confederate general Richard Ewell's corps worshipped here during the Confederate occupation of Carlisle in June 1863. Many renovations and expansions have occurred through the years, including moving the tower to the west end.

On November 28, 1832, a petition was signed by 77 members of the First Presbyterian Church to separate from that church and form the Second Presbyterian Church on April 8, 1833. The separation was due to different philosophies concerning old and new Calvinism. The church seen at right was erected on the southeast corner of South Hanover and West Pomfret Streets. Its architect was John Trautwine, and the church was dedicated in May 1834. This building was demolished in 1870 to provide space for the new church seen below. It was dedicated on May 29, 1873. In the 1970s, the congregation decided to relocate outside the downtown area, and the last service at this church was held on September 19, 1971. The building was later razed. The new church is located at 528 Garland Drive.

The Grace United Methodist Church began in 1893 as the Grace United Brethren Church. The first church structure, seen above, was erected at 24 West South Street at a cost of $2,200 and was dedicated on January 14, 1844. Due to a growing congregation, a larger church was needed. In 1919, the congregation purchased the Emory Methodist Episcopal Church on the northeast corner of West and Pomfret Streets. This building was torn down, and a new church was constructed and dedicated in March 1921. The new structure held the Sunday school. A new church, seen below, providing seating for 550 worshippers, was completed and dedicated on September 28, 1930. Many renovations and additions have been made through the years. After two denominational mergers, the church was renamed in 1968 as Grace United Methodist Church.

Conrad Bucher organized the First United Church of Christ in 1763, which was then known as the German Reformed Church. The first church was located between 142 and 154 South Hanover Street. In 1807, a second church was built beyond West Street, which was where the first Sunday school in Cumberland County was formed. In 1828, a third church, seen at right, was erected on the southeast corner of High and Pitt Streets. This building was not satisfactory for the congregation and was sold to the Methodist Church. With the proceeds from this sale, the fourth church was built in the 1830s at 63–67 West Louther Street, seen below, and the name was changed to the First Reformed Church.

In 1918, the land at 30 North Pitt Street, which was originally where the old post office stood, was purchased for the site of a fifth church building. In April 1924, a new church structure was dedicated for the First Reformed Church, seen above. The mortgage was paid in full in 1944. Later, a tower was erected, shown below. Through the years, other renovations were performed. In 1960, the church merged with the Congregational Christian Churches and changed its name to the First United Church of Christ. In 1983, the building was expanded toward West Louther Street. This expansion included the additions of a social room, a kitchen, and additional classrooms, which are partially underground. The congregation is still active after 256 years.

The Bethel African Methodist Episcopal Church began in 1820. In 1828, a one-story brick church was constructed on East Pomfret Street. It was the first African American church in Carlisle, and it also provided the first school for black children in the area. Sarah Bell, a white woman, was the teacher for about 50 years. The church was a refuge for the Underground Railroad, with John Peck as the conductor. The building, seen above at 127 East Pomfret Street, was constructed in 1867 and remodeled in 1919 and 1930. The church parsonage at 131 East Pomfret Street was built in 1888. Below is an interior photograph of the church; unfortunately, the date is not known. The church was badly damaged in 1947 by a fire, but renovations were completed later that year.

St. Paul Evangelical Lutheran Church was chartered as the Second German Evangelical Lutheran Church on September 8, 1854. The congregation wanted to retain the use of the German language in its services. The first church was at the northwest corner of East Pomfret and South Bedford Streets, seen at left. This building had previously been the German Lutheran Church. In 1896, Pastor Harry B. Strock convinced the congregation to use the English language and to move to the western side of Carlisle. At this time, the name was changed to St. Paul Evangelical Lutheran Church. In 1898, the congregation moved to the corner of West and Louther Streets. The present church, seen below, was built in 1907 by architects George and Edgar Hemminger.

The interior of the St. Paul Evangelical Lutheran Church is seen above. In the early 1900s, the congregation purchased and renovated the old Gobin Armory of the Pennsylvania National Guard, seen below, as a fellowship hall. It was named Strock Hall after their pastor, Harry B. Strock. Pastor Strock had performed his duties for 40 years when he passed the leadership to Rev. Elmer Truchses. Later, a larger educational facility was needed, requiring the construction of the Truchses Educational Building. In April 1991, the congregation installed four church bells, which, in addition to calling the services, sounded the time every hour.

African Methodist Episcopal Zion Church was organized in 1863. The first church was a small stone building on Chapel Avenue between Pitt and Hanover Streets. The second church was located on Dickinson Avenue between Hanover and Pitt Streets. The third church was constructed on West North Street and was dedicated on March 24, 1867. This building later became the Masonic Hall. The congregation used this building for 16 years. In 1883, property was purchased at 134 South West Street. This stone structure, seen here, had been a Presbyterian Sunday school. The building is reputed to have been part of the Underground Railroad and was used as a hospital during the Civil War. In 1909, a brick front and belfry were added to the church, as seen in this photograph. The lovely stained-glass windows, which were not in the original plans, have been added over the years as gifts in honor and in memory of past patrons of the church.

The original building at the corner of West High and Pitt Streets was erected about 1828 by the German Reformed Congregation. It was sold to the Methodist Episcopal Church in 1836 for $5,000. In 1876, the Methodists demolished the structure and erected the brick building seen above. It was known as the Centenary Methodist Church. In 1889, the Methodists sold the building to the Coyle brothers, who divided it into two sections for commercial businesses, as seen below. Over the years, a multitude of businesses such as drugstores and grocery stores used the building. In the 1920s, the Carlisle Commercial College was upstairs. In December 1999, a fire caused heavy damage to the building as well as two other structures, including four businesses. The building was renovated, and today, it continues to offer space for businesses and apartments.

The First Church of God used Sipes Hall for its services in 1894. In November of that year, the congregation purchased the building at 42–44 West Louther Street for $4,500, and held its first service there on December 2, 1894. The building was originally used by St. Paul Evangelical Lutheran Church. This is a view of the second-floor chapel. In 1920, the church building was expanded in the rear, in addition to a new roof and other needed repairs. In 1935, more land was purchased to expand both to the west and to the south of the original building. In 1940, additional renovations were performed, and in 1956, further expansion was completed. In 1970, the congregation decided that a new building was needed. A new church was constructed at 705 Glendale Street. The last service held on West Louther Street was on August 11, 1974. The building on West Louther Street was torn down, and the current post office was constructed on the site.

Two

COMMUNITY ORGANIZATIONS

Court was first held in Carlisle on July 23, 1751, in a temporary log structure. In 1765, a brick building was erected. In 1803, an annex was built to provide county offices, as seen here. Behind the courthouse, another annex was built in 1820 to house the fire apparatus. The borough council met on the second floor. On March 24, 1845, this building was destroyed by an arson fire.

After the first courthouse of Cumberland County burned down, the one at left was built in 1846 by Daniel Wilt and Samuel Bryan Jr. It has a brick exterior with a sandstone portico, modified Corinthian capitals, and a bell and clock tower. This courthouse was under siege by Confederate forces in 1863, and some of the damage can still be seen. The building has undergone very little renovations and preserves its mid-19th-century features. The county offices outgrew the space, and a new courthouse was built in 1961, as seen below. It is across the street from the 1846 structure on the site of the old market house. It was designed by the firm of Lawrie and Green.

The first jail was built in 1753 at the northwest corner of East High and North Bedford Streets. It was used for 100 years before being taken down. The jail seen here was built on the same site in 1854 and designed by architect Edward Haviland. The builders were Myers and Gutshall. It was built of limestone with a facade of brown sandstone. It has a two-floor design with an open center and an iron stairway at one end. It contained apartments for the sheriff and his family and offices for the keeper. The capacity was 96 inmates, but it frequently exceeded that. There was a segregated section for female inmates. Due to overcrowding and structural violations, a new prison was constructed, and this building was vacated on May 15, 1985. The building was renovated and is still used for county offices.

The Bosler Library was dedicated on January 30, 1900. J. Herman Bosler bequeathed $20,000 for the building of this structure. It was built by A.H. Brindle, and has a marble front and four Ionic columns. Renovations and additions were performed in the interior throughout the years, but the exterior of this building has remained intact. In 1909, the circulation was 25,048 books. The two buildings to the right of this on West High Street were purchased and torn down to allow for expansion. The first expansion was in 1987 and then again in 1993. The needs of the library continued to grow, requiring other renovations in 2000 and in 2013. This library is part of the Cumberland County Library System. There are seven libraries throughout the county to serve its growing population.

A centrally located market was considered essential to the town. A location for a market place was in the original plan for Carlisle. The first actual structure was built in 1802, but it was a basic shed with a roof and no walls. The second structure was similar and was built in 1836, as seen above. At the same location, the southeast corner of the square, the building seen below was built in 1878 and was a 30-foot-high brick structure. It cost $40,000. On the second floor were the borough offices. At one time, there were 146 stalls for rent. One vendor occupied the same stall for more than 60 years. The last day of market was November 28, 1951. After a court battle, the beloved market house was torn down to make room for the new courthouse.

The Cumberland Fire Company was organized in February 1809. The Union and Cumberland companies shared space in the town hall until it burned in 1845. Cumberland then moved to a one-story building at 32 South Bedford Street. In 1860, the borough deeded this land to Cumberland, and the company constructed a two-story building, which it used until 1896, when the three-story structure at 121 East Louther Street at left was erected. The bay door was widened in 1947 to accommodate larger fire apparatus (below). The bell tower and the balcony were removed in 1957. In 1974, fire damaged the firehouse and killed two members, and the station was rebuilt. In 1984, Cumberland merged with the Good Will Fire Company and became the Cumberland Good Will Fire Company. The company relocated with the Good Will Fire Company on West Ridge Street.

Good Will Fire Company was formed in 1855 for the purpose of laying out the hose for the engine companies. However, it soon acquired its own hand engine. Around 1857, the company built a firehouse on East Pomfret Street, seen at right. In 1870, the company built a three-story firehouse at 22 South Hanover Street. The third floor of this building was used as the Masonic Hall. The building was renovated in 1894 to hold fire hoses. In 1908, Good Will sold the building and relocated to the rear of 30–32 South Hanover Street. In 1913, it moved to a new station at 161 West Pomfret Street, seen below. It was formerly the home of F.C. Bosler, and was totally refitted. In 1966, Good Will moved to 102 West Ridge Street, and in 1984, the company merged with the Cumberland Fire Company.

The Empire Hook and Ladder Company was formed as the Pioneer Hook and Ladder Company in January 1859, but was soon renamed Empire. Its first building was completed in November 1859 at Dickinson Avenue and Pitt Street. In 1868, a new firehouse was built at 38 West Pomfret Street, pictured above. There was no bell in the cupola and no alarm system until 1920. In 1931, using the architectural firm Bobb and Todd, the entire front brick wall was replaced with architectural concrete and the entrance was widened. The firehouse, in an Art Deco style, is seen at right. In 1991, the company combined with the Friendship Fire Company to form the Empire Friendship Firefighters Association. A new building was constructed on Spring Road in 1996. In 2006, the association formally changed its name to Carlisle Fire Rescue Services.

The Union Fire Company was organized on April 6, 1789. Its equipment was first housed in a building near the courthouse. In 1821, a two-story town hall and firehouse was built beside the courthouse. This building was destroyed, along with the courthouse, during the fire of 1845. The fire company relocated to 34 West Louther Street in a one-story frame structure built in 1845. In 1859, this firehouse was replaced with the two-story brick building seen at right. The bell was installed in 1878, and the building was expanded in 1879. In 1888, property was purchased across the road at 35 West Louther Street, and a new firehouse was built to celebrate the company's centennial, as seen below. In 1961, the front was reconstructed to allow larger apparatus, and in 1977, a large two-story addition was built.

Hamilton School was named after James Hamilton Jr., the first secretary of the school board and an influential Carlisle resident. The property at 69 East Pomfret Street was first purchased for a school building, and it originally had two frame structures. In 1868, the building pictured here was erected. It accommodated four classrooms, two on each floor. This layout was used until it closed in 1936.

A school was established in 1849 at 43 North Pitt Street to house two classrooms. In 1886, the building shown here was erected, and the school was named Lincoln School. It was a two-story building with four classrooms: primary, secondary, grammar, and high. In 1890, the building was used for African American students, and the white students were moved to the new Wilson School. It closed in 1927, and the building was sold to the Knights of Pythias.

Wilson School was named after James Wilson, signer of the Declaration of Independence. The brick building seen here was erected at 101 West North Street in 1890 and designed as the new segregated coed high school for whites. It continued as a high school until 1927, when it became an elementary school for African American students until 1949, when the schools were fully desegregated. The school was razed in the 1970s.

Penn School was erected in 1897 at 121 North Bedford Street. It was a two-story brick building designed to house grammar and high schools. It originally had a large assembly room and seven classrooms. In 1899, the high school was moved to Franklin School on Walnut Street. The grammar school remained here until 1928, when it was moved to Lambertson High School on Graham Street. Today, the building is apartments.

The Hamilton Library Association was chartered in 1874 and is believed to be the oldest county historical society in the state. This building was a gift from the estate of James Hamilton Jr. and was erected in 1881. The photograph at left shows the building in the 1930s. In 1966, a fireproof addition was constructed, which included a large museum and meeting room. In 1972, an additional wing was built. The museum has a great collection of Cumberland County memorabilia, including one of the three printing presses on which Continental paper currency was printed, and George Washington's Masonic apron. The photograph below shows an exhibit of artifacts on display during Carlisle's 1901 sesquicentennial. The library has a huge collection of historic books and archival information available for historical and genealogical research.

On the public square, beside the old courthouse, is Veterans Memorial Courtyard, dedicated to all veterans of Cumberland County. This includes a number of memorials. The largest is the memorial to veterans who died in the Civil War, which is seen here. There are 17 officers and 325 enlisted men recognized. Other memorials recognize veterans from the Vietnam War, World War II, those who lost their lives during the First World War, and the Medal of Honor recipients of Cumberland County. Ten recipients are cited on the Medal of Honor memorial. There is also a memorial in recognition of the athletic achievements of Jim Thorpe, who was a student at the Carlisle Indian School. The most unusual memorial is a large in-ground gold medallion recognizing the creation of the Forbes Trail, which crossed over 300 miles of Pennsylvania and was part of the westward movement starting from Cumberland County.

The main graveyard in Carlisle is on South Street. It is known as the Old Graveyard. Its oldest marker is from 1757. It is the final resting place of a number of significant residents of Carlisle. At left is John Bannister Gibson, who was chief justice of the Pennsylvania Supreme Court for 24 years. Other judicial leaders include Chief Justice Hugh Brackenridge, Judge Frederick Watts, and Judge John Reed. Some Revolutionary War veterans buried here include Gen. John Armstrong, Gen. John Armstrong Jr., Gen. Samuel Alexander, and Brig. Gen. William Thompson, who was the first commissioned officer of the Continental army. There are also at least 550 veterans from the Civil War. Below is a view of the graveyard.

Mary Biddle purchased the two properties on the corner of East High and East Streets in 1885. In 1887, she founded the Female Benevolent Society to help women. This building at 175 East High Street was constructed in 1893. It was intended to be a women's home but was used as the first hospital in Carlisle until 1896, when it was returned to its original purpose. The home was founded by Biddle and named as a memorial to her sister Lydia Baird. The money from the rental of the property on the corner, 177 East High Street, was used to support the home. Biddle bequeathed the home to the Female Benevolent Society in 1901 to continue to help women. The home had 10 guestrooms, and in 1921, electric lighting was installed. In 1947, a sink with hot and cold water was installed in each room. The home continued in operation until March 1984, when six residents were moved to the Todd Home on Mooreland Avenue.

The Carlisle Aerie 1299 of the Fraternal Order of Eagles was formed in 1906 with 60 members. In 1909, the order purchased the property at left for $6,000. Prior to this, the building served as a home. Through the years, the Aerie added to and renovated its building many times, including the 1938 installation of four bowling alleys in the basement. As the years passed, six more alleys were added. The Aerie has sponsored many local, state, and national charities through the years. For over 70 years, it has sponsored a little league baseball team in Carlisle and other locations. The photograph below shows the building as it is today.

The Carlisle Young Women's Christian Association (YWCA) was founded in January 1919. Later in 1919, the organization purchased the property at 15 West High Street. This was originally the home of John Herman Bosler from the mid-1800s until 1915, when his wife, Mary Jane, died. The house was renovated to accommodate the needs of the YWCA. During the renovations, a schedule was developed that allowed the women partial use of the facilities of the Young Men's Christian Association (YMCA) at 27 West High Street. By 1920, the building improvements were completed, and the women had access to their own gymnasium with lockers and showers, a cafeteria, kitchen, and dormitory rooms. The Red Cross Chapter Office was also located in this building. By 1973, the YWCA had relocated to 311 South West Street.

This structure at 27 West High Street was known as the Douglas Building when it was originally constructed, but it is most remembered as the YMCA. As seen at left, it was a three-story building with two storefronts on the first floor. These were Lesher's Tailor Shop and Eckels Insurance and Real Estate in 1908. In 1929, it was enlarged by adding a fourth story, and the facade was changed to what is seen below. The first floor had a gymnasium, game rooms, and six bowling alleys. The second floor had an auditorium that could hold 265 people. The third and fourth floors housed 27 sleeping rooms. In 1965, the YMCA moved to a larger facility in the renovated Franklin School Building on West Street.

The Independent Order of Odd Fellows (IOOF) in Carlisle organized in 1843. The lodge's first home was on South Hanover Street, in the Beetem residence. In 1858, the IOOF moved to the Trout Building on 31 West High Street; William Trout had constructed the three-story brick structure. The lodge purchased the building in 1895 and began making improvements in 1899. The building had three storefronts on the first floor. One of the stores was Lute Halbert's Cigar and Pool Room. In 1904, Halbert added a four-lane bowling alley in the back. Another store was W.K. Piper's Book Store, and the third was the Chocolate Shop, which dated to 1846. The second floor held offices used by county officials, and the lodge room was on the third floor. In 1928, for their 85th anniversary, the Odd Fellows gave the building a new facade in a Neo-Gothic style, as seen here.

The American Legion Home Post No. 101 in Carlisle had its first meeting on August 4, 1919, at the armory, which was built in 1881. The above photograph of the armory shows Company G, 8th Regiment of the Pennsylvania National Guard in 1919. The Ladies Auxiliary Unit was formed in 1922. By 1929, the post's membership was already at 369, and the auxiliary had 167 members. In the early 1950s, the American Legion relocated to 138 North Hanover Street, and the armory was sold to St. Paul Evangelical Lutheran Church. The American Legion shared the building with Braund's Pharmacy. In 1961, the Legion moved to its present location at 142–146 North Hanover Street, seen below.

Three

Downtown Businesses

The Opera House was built in 1897. The grand opening show was *El Captain* in September 1898. The main floor had seating for 650, with 550 seats in the horseshoe balcony and 200 more in the gallery. In 1908, it began showing movies. In 1925, it became the Strand Theater after extensive improvements. After a fire in 1972, the building was demolished.

This building at 2 North Hanover Street was constructed in 1915 by Jacob Weiner. He and his brother Albert sold men's clothing. The Wieners stayed in this location until 1926. In 1928, Swigert's Men Shop opened here and closed in 1960. In the 1960s, the Hamilton House Men's Clothing Store moved here. Later, it became an art and gift shop.

In the 1880s, Samuel A. Haverstick built this structure at 8–10 North Hanover Street for his drugstore and later a dry goods store. When Haverstick died in 1910, his son Samuel W. took over the building for his stationery and notions shop. A fire destroyed the structure in 1924, but Samuel W. rebuilt his business. In 1933, the W.T. Grant Company moved to this address and remained here until 1966.

Originally, the brick building seen above on the left was owned by Charley Sipe and referred to as Sipe Hall. He operated a shoe store here in the early 1900s. Later, Harvey Mentzer bought the property and changed the facade. There were now two storefronts. The left side was used by the F.W. Woolworth Company when it opened in 1910. The right side was used by Bowman and Company. Next to Bowman's was the Berg Building, owned by Herman Berg and later Charles Berg and featuring men's clothing. In March 1924, a large fire destroyed the Mentzer and Berg Buildings, as seen below. The Mentzer was rebuilt as the Woolworth Building. The Berg Building was reconstructed with a stone facade and continued to use the same name.

The Berg Building, which was originally in this location, was reconstructed after the 1924 fire and continued as a men's clothing store at 22–24 North Hanover Street until 1937. In that year, the Carlisle Meat Market moved in. The photograph above shows the Carlisle Meat Market at the 22–24 North Hanover Street location. In 1942, the business changed its name to the Carlisle Food Market and continued in this location until 1952, when it moved to its new building at 100 North Hanover Street. The Carlisle Food Market was later bought by Giant Food Store. In 1955, Endicott Johnson Shoe Company, seen at left, took over the building at 22–24 North Hanover Street and continued operating here until 1964.

The above photograph shows the F.W. Woolworth Company in 1930 on North Hanover Street. This building was constructed after the 1924 fire that destroyed the previous Woolworth's store. At this time, the building was shared with two other businesses. To the right of Woolworth's was the Carlisle Meat Market. At far right was Rosen's Sample Shop, which sold ladies' accessories. Both moved in 1937. At that time, Woolworth's expanded and used the entire first floor of the building (below). The second and third floors were apartments. Woolworth's continued at this location until 1997.

J.L. Weibley Grocery Store, seen above, was at 26 North Hanover Street from about 1905 until 1920. In 1922, Peter Garber bought the property and established a shoe store. Garber operated his business here for two years. In 1926, he leased the building to Kinney Shoe Store (left). In 1929, Garber sold the property to Paul E. Dutrey, who leased it to Kinney Shoe Store until 1936, when the company moved across the street to 15 North Hanover Street. At that time, Paul Dutrey opened Dutrey's Shoe Store, which he had been operating in his parents' home.

John and Maime Dutrey lived in the home seen above at right at 51 West Louther Street. Originally, they sold used furniture, and Dutrey was an auctioneer. However, in 1922, their son Paul began selling shoes on the first floor of this house. After he bought the 26 North Hanover Street property, he eventually moved the business to that location, as seen at right. Paul's son Richard became the owner in 1953 and enlarged the store. In 1957, Chico the monkey came to live in the store and entertained young customers. Paul died in 1962, and Chico died two months later of a broken heart. Dutrey's Shoe Store closed in 2006.

Moses Blumenthal opened Blumenthal Men's Clothing Store in 1901 at 32 North Hanover Street. This photograph is from 1933. When Blumenthal died in 1948, his son Richard continued the business. In 1966, Richard retired and sold the business to James Wardecker, an employee since 1942. Wardecker died in 1998, and his son Fred continues to operate the clothing business in the same location today.

The Bon Ton millinery store opened in 1909 at 36 North Hanover Street. It sold hats, furs, and ladies' wear. In 1913, the company moved across the street, and the J.H. Troupe music store took over the property. Troupe closed in the early 1920s. In 1928, Israel's Men's Wear opened at this location and continued until 1942, when it moved to 107 North Hanover Street.

This corner property was known as Meck's Corner, as seen at the top of the building at right above. A grocery store occupied it in the 1890s. The photograph above is from 1909, when the building was the location of a John S. Low wholesale dealer in fine liquors, wines, brandies, gin, and cordials until Prohibition. In 1924, the Atlantic and Pacific Tea Company (A&P) occupied the building and continued until 1940. At that time, Wenger's Women Clothing Store, as seen at right, took over the property until the 1970s. Today, the property is occupied by Carlisle Kung Fu.

The Carlisle Bank received a charter in 1813. Originally, the bank rented rooms, but in 1816, a new building was purchased for $11,000. This building, seen above, was at 3 North Hanover Street and provided continuous banking services until its charter expired in 1846. At this time, a charter was issued to the Carlisle Deposit Bank and Trust Company at the same location; Carlisle Deposit bought the building for $4,500. In 1884, the first telephone was installed, and in 1890, a larger vault was installed to meet the increased business and provide safety deposit boxes. The bank is seen below in 1909. After various mergers and transfers, the bank closed in 2007. Today, the building, called The Vault, is used as a special events venue.

The large brick structure at right was the Gardner Building. It had two storefronts, with Bowman and Company on the left in the early 1900s and Weiner Brothers, a men's clothing store, on the right (below). This was Bowman's first location in Carlisle. The Gardner Building was destroyed by fire in 1933. The iron railing on the front was used on the windows of the Hamilton Library of the Cumberland County Historical Society. After the fire, the Montgomery Ward company purchased the property and built a new structure on the site of the Gardner Building.

The Home Theater, Carlisle's first moving picture house, was at 19 North Hanover Street, as seen at left. The theater opened in February 1913 and could seat 900 people. It only operated here until 1915. In 1916, Bowman and Company moved to this location and made some modifications to the front facade, as seen below. The windows on the second and third floors advertised linoleum, rugs, carpets, mattings, coats, a ladies' department, and suits. Bowman and Company continued here until 1926, when it moved to 10–16 South Hanover Street. This building became the first local home for the J.C. Penney company, which operated here until 1959.

This property was originally known as Halbert's Corner, after C.L. Halbert, who lived here in the 1860s. The Charles Shapley family purchased the property at 37 North Hanover Street around 1876. The photograph above shows the Shapley furniture store in the 1880s. The business operated here until 1924. In 1925, Gus Giannaris bought the property and opened the Texas Restaurant here (right). Through the years, various Greek proprietors operated the restaurant and continued to serve the popular Texas hot dog until it closed in 1997. After a few years, the Lone Star Restaurant opened at this location. Today, it is the North Hanover Grille.

The building shown here at 117 North Hanover Street is the J.C. Penney department store. In 1959, J.C. Penney moved from the 19 North Hanover Street location and opened this new store. This location had previously been used by Eggert and Finkelstein Cleaners and Dyers, which later became Finkelstein and Sons Cleaners. J.C. Penney continued here until 1978, when it moved to a shopping center.

This is the building on North Hanover Street in which Sheaffer Brothers began in the late 1910s. Chester, James, Nelson, and David Sheaffer sold automobile accessories and provided tire services such as vulcanizing, retreading, and recapping. The business grew, and in the late 1950s, the brothers began selling sporting goods.

Steele's Café at 200 North Hanover Street is seen here. It was also known as Steele's Beer Garden. The café started at this location in 1936. Before that, it was the location of the Wagner Hardware Company, which started here in 1924. Steele's Café continued here until 1972.

The building at 138 North Hanover Street was the location of Kunkel's Drug Store from 1906 through 1936. Willis George Kunkel was the pharmacist and lived above the store. Judson N. Davids Drugs took over the building from 1938 until the early 1940s. After that, Braund's Pharmacy started here, and until 1961 shared the building with the American Legion. Braund's continued here until the late 1960s.

Samuel Kronenberg opened his clothing store in 1866 at 4 South Hanover Street, next to the Franklin House. In 1893, Kronenberg died, and the business was taken over by his two sons, William and Edward. In 1906, they erected a new building, seen at left in 1910, on the site of the original stone structure. With the expansion of the business in 1916, the sons purchased the Franklin House and demolished both buildings to erect a new, larger structure on the two lots. This building was destroyed by fire in 1929. In 1930, Edward Kronenberg immediately erected a new building, shown below in the 1930s. The store closed in 1981.

Montgomery Ward opened its first store in Carlisle in 1928 at 164 North Hanover Street. In the late 1930s, the business moved to its new building, seen above, at 9–13 North Hanover Street. Montgomery Ward continued here until 1965, when it moved into a shopping mall outside of town. At that time, the Bon-Ton department store took over the building, as seen below. Bon-Ton operated here for 11 years, until 1977. Like Montgomery Ward, it moved to a shopping center outside of town.

G.W. Rinesmith's Sons parade float is seen in front of the business at 114 North Hanover Street. The parade was part of the 1909 Old Home Week celebration. George Rinesmith began his stove and tinware store in 1864, as the banner states. His sons Clayton and Harry continued the business after their father's death. By 1924, Earley's furniture store was located here and continued until 1970.

This building at 113 North Hanover Street was known for its restaurants. In the 1900s, Casper Eckert had his restaurant and ice cream parlor here. In the 1920s and 1930s, the building was a grocery store and later a fruit market. In the 1940s, the Mayflower Restaurant began here and continued until the 1960s. From 1965 through 1972, the Broiler restaurant was here.

In 1887, J.W. Plank started a retail clothing store at 10 South Hanover Street. He enlarged the business, as seen above in 1901. Plank also owned the Carlisle Garment Factory at 44–46 North Bedford Street ,where he manufactured ladies and children's wear. The photograph below shows women working there. J.W. Plank was one of the first in the country to create ready-made dresses. In the early 1900s, he changed the name of the store to Imperial Dry Goods Company. By 1920, he had moved to Philadelphia, and the Imperial Dry Goods Company closed in 1922. The store was purchased by Bowman and Company in 1926.

Bowman and Company was started in Carlisle in 1901 by Samuel Bowman and his partner Albert Stecher. Bowman died in 1910, at which time Stecher took Samuel Hertzler as a partner. In the 1920s, Stecher retired and was replaced by Albert Watson, who became the sole proprietor when Hertzler retired in 1929. After moving many times, the company purchased the property at 10 South Hanover Street. In 1926, this was the largest store with the highest purchase price in Carlisle—$100,000. Bowman's was known for its pneumatic tubes, seen above, that moved money to and from the sales areas to the central office. The photograph below shows the store in 1960. On December 9, 1962, a fire destroyed Bowman and Company and McCrory's store and damaged other businesses in the block. Today, a hotel is on this site.

The building seen above at 20 South Hanover Street was the home of the Carlisle Chamber of Commerce from the early 1900s to about 1948. The chamber had the first-floor facade of the brick building re-faced in stone and added four dramatic Gothic arches. The chamber moved to 112 West High Street and later to 213 South Hanover Street. In addition to providing community services, it promoted all Carlisle businesses, including agriculture, industry, tourism, and retail. In the 1950s, this building was the location of McCrory's five and dime store. The arches were removed, and a large sign was installed (right). McCrory's remained here until the fire in 1962.

The brick building seen above in the 1880s at 22 South Hanover Street was the location of Coyle Brothers Variety Store. The business was started in the 1870s by Samuel and William Coyle. The Coyle wagon is covered with advertisements of the items the company sold, such as a variety of cotton fabrics, horse and cattle powder, and wallpaper. In 1900, Charles A. Parkinson's furniture store, seen below, was located here. Parkinson made, sold, and delivered furniture. Unfortunately, he died suddenly in 1901 and the business closed. In 1910, Cochran and Alcock, later Cochran and Allen hardware store, took over the property.

Cochran and Allen hardware started in 1879 as Stevick and Barr. It was first located at 1 South Hanover Street and moved to various other locations. The company changed its name five times. It moved to the property at 22 South Hanover Street in 1910. The business was named Cochran and Alcock from 1902 until 1921. In 1921, the name changed to Cochran and Allen after the new proprietors, A. Max Cochran and M.W. Allen (right). This was the place to go for hardware of all varieties. Through the years, the facade was changed, as seen below. The company remained in business until 1991. This building remains today and is the downtown location of Orrstown Bank.

From 1912 to 1917, the building at 5 South Hanover Street was the location of the Lucretia Williams Shop, which sold clothing for women and children. In the 1920s, the A&P food store moved here. The photograph above shows the A&P in 1940. It was on the left side of the Molly Pitcher Hotel. In the 1950s, the A&P moved to the right side of the hotel, at 17 South Hanover Street, as seen at left. This building was larger, and the grocery store was the most modern in Carlisle when it opened, with seven checkout lanes.

Jacob E. Trimmer opened Trimmer's five and dime store at 17 South Hanover Street and a variety store at 25 South Hanover Street in the 1920s. The stores were essentially one, as seen above, but the 1920s directories listed them separately. In 1952, Trimmer moved his store to the corner of South and Hanover Streets, as seen below. This location had a long line of grocery stores dating to the Civil War. Trimmer continued the tradition by opening a grocery store here. In 1960, after the death of Jacob Trimmer, the three-story building was sold to Lester Kingsborough, and the one-story annex was sold to Harold Cline.

The Carlisle Trust Company, seen above at 2 West High Street, received its charter on October 4, 1905. In 1909, this bank became the first in the nation to offer a Christmas club, a short-term program for saving money for Christmas. It was developed by the bank's treasurer, Merkel Landis. In 1938, it was one of the first banks to offer mortgage financing under the Federal Housing Administration. Also, after World War II, it started a veterans' program called GI lending. Through the years, the Carlisle Trust Company became the Dauphin Deposit Bank. In 1960, the building was remodeled, and the third floor was removed. The Eyers Building next door was razed, and a new structure was constructed on that site and incorporated into the original bank, as seen below.

In 1811, Archibald Loudon bookseller and print shop was located at 10–12 West High Street. In the 1890s, this was the location of the Bursk hat shop. By 1900, Samuel E. Weaver's tailor shop occupied the building, as seen at right. After this, the Altland dyeing and cleaning company was located here, with the Republican party headquarters on the second floor. In 1933, the Palace confectionery was located at 10 West High Street. In 1961, Cappiello Insurance joined the Palace at 12 West High Street, as seen below. The Palace had a soda fountain in addition to a wide assortment of candies. By 1969, George Faller's law office was located here, and the building's facade was radically changed. In 1970, the building was reconstructed due to damage from a major fire.

This large, three-story brick building was constructed by Jason Eby in 1851 and was named Marion Hall in honor of Revolutionary general Francis Marion. At the time, Marion Hall was Carlisle's principal performing stage, with seating for 500 people. In 1857, the owner converted the hall into rooms for businesses. From 1896 through 1902, Joseph Ogilby sold groceries, china, lamps, and onyx tables here, and Benjamin Emrick's drug store shared the building. In 1909, the building was used by Jacob Livingston grocery and delicatessen and William Shearer's drug store, as seen here. The building was damaged in a 1970 fire. This structure and the old Cumberland Valley Savings and Loan building were torn down, and a new Cumberland Valley Savings and Loan was erected. It is now the location of the Dennis Marion Public Services Building.

Horn's Drug Store was on West High Street in 1911. Dr. Wilbur Horn began his drugstore in the 1880s at 28 West High Street, and lived next door at 26 West High Street. He ran the drugstore until his death in 1937. Finkelstein Cleaners used this location in the 1940s. By 1955, Gaynor's millinery store was here, seen below. Gaynor's sold hats and handbags and continued to operate until 1967. In that year, Helen's Hat Shop moved into this building and continued at this location until 1972.

Three buildings were demolished to construct the Comerford Theatre. The first, at 36 West High Street, was the Samuel McClellan home until 1936 (above). The second was at 38–40 West High Street (left) in 1920. At the time, it was the Dickinson barbershop and shoe shine parlor. A poolroom was accessible through the archway on the right. Among the many services offered by the barbershop was "electric hat cleaning." In 1924, Charles Link's bakery was here, and in 1930, it was the Sweetheart Shoppe selling confectionery goodies. It was owned by Wilbur Amos. From 1933 to 1938, Terris, the Hatter was here.

The third building demolished for the Comerford Theatre was at 42–44 West High Street, seen above in 1910. At the time, it was John and Mary Ploughs' Millinery. In the 1920s, John Plough switched to selling real estate at this location, and the Cumberland Valley Telephone Company shared the building. The Comerford Theatre was opened in 1939. It was built in the Art Deco style and had 1,400 seats. The name was changed to the Carlisle Theatre in 1950. There were businesses located in both wings of the building, as seen below in 1961. The theater closed in 1986. It was renovated in 1991 and opened as a multipurpose movie and performing arts center.

From the 1860s to the 1880s, the third building from the right at left, at 50 West High Street, was the home of the Edward Biddle family. Later, it housed a number of restaurants, and from 1907 to 1952, the Smith Music House was located here selling music-related items and appliances. In 1961, as seen below, it was the location of Wilson's Drugs, which closed in 1972. Later, it was the New York Deli. In 1999, it was destroyed along with two additional buildings by a fire started by the owner of the deli, who was sentenced to 30 years in prison for arson.

Thomas Conlyn established a jewelry store in the first block of West High Street in 1839. His son Robert took over the business and moved the store to 139 West High Street (right). He operated the store until Thomas L. Gray bought the business in 1917. The name remained Conlyn Jewelry Store, and it continued at this location, with Chester B. Gray taking over for his father, until 1951. The photograph below shows the interior of the store. The Endicott Johnson Shoe Store took over the location in 1953 but only remained until 1955. At that time, Patty's Pastry Shop and Luncheonette opened here and remained until 1960.

The Farmers Bank of Carlisle was granted a charter in 1868. In 1902, the bank reorganized and received a new charter as the Farmers Trust Company at 1 West High Street, seen above. This building was owned by Robert Given, the first president. The bank rented the first floor, and the Given family lived in the upper floors. In 1916, the bank bought the building for $30,000. Renovations were made throughout the years, but in 1961, the bank made major improvements and expanded the building to the north, as seen below. In 1982, the bank reorganized into the Financial Trust Corporation, and in 1997 as the Keystone Financial Company. Today, it is the Merchants and Trust Bank.

The Orpheum Theatre was built in 1909 and could seat 500 patrons. It was used for vaudeville and moving pictures. The theater replaced the home of James Hamilton Jr., seen at right, who originally owned this half of the block of West High Street. The large arched front of the theater can be seen above on the left during the parade for Jim Thorpe and Louis Tewania's return from the 1912 Olympics. The theater was destroyed in a fire in November 1939. It was not rebuilt, and at one point, the lot was used to sell used cars. Now it is part of the parking lot for the Cumberland County Historical Society and is enclosed by a decorative gate.

The Stuart Building, seen above, was a three-story structure on the north side of West High Street that had at least two storefronts. In this 1901 photograph, it was occupied by the Carlisle Post Office and Totton's Cigar Store and was decorated for Carlisle's sesquicentennial. James Totton also had a bowling alley in his cigar store. By 1909, the post office remained, but it was now Brady's Cigar and Billiards, operated by George W. Brady. The building is shown at left decorated for Old Home Week in 1909. From 1938 until 1981, this was the location of Femina Restaurant.

In the early 1900s, the Zug brothers had a men's clothing store in this corner building. Williamson Linn McCullough purchased the corner building and later all the structures up to the Orpheum Theatre. In 1909, he made all the buildings four-story, and they were held together with one roofline and a large decorative pediment that read "McCullough Block." Later, Bolen Company purchased the property. Shown above around 1920, the Sugar Bowl, Coney Island Quick Lunch, and the Dickinsonian Café occupied the building. In 1937, the corner spot was the location of the A&P. In 1938, the Hamilton restaurant opened at the corner location. In 1961, the Hamilton was enlarged and took over the adjacent storefront, as seen at right. It is still operating today and is the home of the famous "Hotchee Dog."

The four dormered buildings above were constructed in the 18th century. Second from the right was J.E. Pague's grocery store, and the next was empty. At far left was a shop that sold tobacco, cigars, and oysters. These three were razed in the 1890s to construct the Henderson Building, seen below. Pague continued to have a store on the right side of this building, at 10 East High Street. Frederick & Company plumbers occupied 12 East High Street. G.T. McIntire's clothing store was on the left at 14 East High Street. The stone building at far right remained intact. Today, the first-floor windows of the Henderson Building have been bricked over, and it is used for offices.

This house at 35 East High Street was built around 1850 by George W. Hitner, a dry goods merchant in Carlisle. He died in 1859. The house had a number of owners until the 1920s, when it was purchased by the Carlisle Gas and Water Company for its offices. The company was originally formed in 1853. By 1888, it also provided electricity to Carlisle. By the 1920s, the use of electricity had increased so much that the company could not handle the need, and in 1922, the Carlisle Gas and Water Company merged with the Pennsylvania Power and Light Company, marking the end of 34 years of being the only local electrical utility in Carlisle. The offices of Pennsylvania Power and Light remained here until 1969.

This property at 36 East High Street has been used in many ways through the years. It began as the home of Judge Thomas Duncan of the Supreme Court of Pennsylvania. He lived in Carlisle for many years, but resided in Philadelphia for his last 10 years. He owned many properties in Carlisle and constructed this building at the corner of East High and Bedford Streets for his son Stephen Duncan. Thomas Duncan died in 1827. After his death, this property was home to a number of families until the early 1900s. The Fraternal Order of Owls used the building as its headquarters from 1909 to 1920. For the rest of the 1920s, it was converted back to a home for James and Augusta McIntosh. In the 1930s, it became the location of Clark M. Keck's restaurant and bar. Keck remained here until 1969, when it was again converted back to a home.

This is B.B. Stearn's jewelry store. Stearn started his business at 9 West High Street, but in the 1940s, relocated to 30 West High Street. He was named Jeweler of the Year in 1968. Brewster Stearn remained in business at this location until 1981. He died in 1991.

Baker's grocery store was at 152 North Hanover Street. Alfred Baker started his business in 1902 after years of farming. He continued the business until he died in 1914. At that time, his son Herman M. Baker took over. Like his father, he continued to operate the grocery store until his death in 1958.

In 1913, at the age of 32, Foster G. Cromleigh began his stationery business at 119 West High Street (above). The 1913 photograph shows that Cromleigh also sold magazines, newspapers, and postcards. Prior to opening the stationery store, he and his wife, Cora, managed the Troy Steam Laundry on North Pitt Street in Carlisle. Around 1924, Cromleigh moved his stationery business down the street to 129 West High Street (left). His store was known as "The Little Store with the Big Stock." He continued operating the store until his death in 1943.

This building was the headquarters for the *American Volunteer* newspaper. It was printed in Carlisle from 1814 through 1909. The above photograph was taken before 1878, when the large Market House was built in the foreground. The photograph below shows the same building in the early 1900s, when it was the location of the Carlisle Commercial College. Men and women attended the college to prepare for a business career. The college taught bookkeeping, shorthand, typing, and penmanship. It relocated in the late 1920s to a structure behind the Kronenberg Building. The Hartzell Book Bindery was then located here. Through the years, the street had different names, including Market House Avenue and Liberty Avenue.

The building above held the *Sentinel* printing office as well as a number of other offices. In 1924, there were four attorney offices, a justice of the peace, a real estate office, an insurance office, and a barbershop in addition to the printing office and newspaper headquarters. The photograph below shows some of the staff in front of the building in 1884. The building facade changed through the years. The *Sentinel* was founded in 1863 in Shippensburg and moved to Carlisle in 1874. In 1953, the building was declared unsafe, and the *Sentinel* moved to North Street. The Dauphin Deposit Bank bought the old building and tore it down for a parking lot. The newspaper continues to serve the community today.

This building at 129 West High Street was constructed around 1830. For part of his life, Rear Adm. Benjamin P. Lamberton, seen below, lived here. Admiral Lamberton was raised in Carlisle and attended Dickinson College. In 1898, he was appointed chief of staff to Commodore George Dewey at the Battle of Manila. He died in Washington, DC, in 1912. At that time, the house was owned by his daughter Mary, who sold the property to Foster Cromleigh. The three lower windows were changed to one large one to accommodate Cromleigh's stationery and book store. Later, it became Light's Stationery Store' today, it is the Whistlestop Book Shop.

The building at 152 West High Street was constructed around 1793. It was the headquarters of *Kline's Gazette*, which was the first newspaper published west of the Susquehanna River. George Kline was the publisher from 1785 to 1810. This photograph was taken around 1960. The building has undergone many changes. The original stone structure is contained inside the current building, and it now has three floors.

This three-story building at 157 North Hanover Street housed Joe the Motorist's Friend. In the early 1920s, it was the location of Charles Hays, electrician contractor. Joe the Motorist's Friend opened at 155 North Hanover Street in 1938 and moved next door in 1942. The business continued to operate here until about 1975.

Four

Residential Homes

This home on North Hanover Street was built by Reverend Steele in the late 1700s. He sold the property to Robert Semple, who converted it into a tavern. In 1794, Gen. Ephraim Blaine purchased the house with plans to build a mansion but instead renovated the building into identical townhouses for his sons Robert and James. Later, it was sold to David Watts. The Watts family lived there for about 70 years.

This house at 141 West High Street was built around 1790. It was purchased by Isaac Brown Parker in 1813. He remodeled the home and virtually rebuilt the front in the Greek Revival style in 1830. The house was used by Mary Johnson Dillon in her novel about Carlisle, *In Olde Bellaire*. Since then, it has been known as the Bellaire House. It remained in the Parker family until 1909, when the Elks Club purchased the property. In 1955, the Elks leased the ground floor to Bruce and Doris Calaman for the Bellaire Restaurant. Later, the Calamans purchased the entire building. The upstairs library and parlor were used as banquet rooms. Raymond and Mary Hall purchased the building in 1970 and continued to operate a restaurant until the 1990s.

This house at the corner of South Hanover and East Pomfret Streets was built around 1896 by Weirich Zollinger Bentz and is one of the few structures in Carlisle in the Richardson Romanesque style. Bentz was well traveled and included many European interior features in the home. In the early 1920s, the house was sold to Frances B. Lefever, the widow of Enos K. Lefever.

This home at 110 South Hanover Street was built between 1890 and 1896 by Edward Beetem, the owner of Carlisle Carpet Mills at 401 East Louther Street. After Beetem's death, it was sold to Joseph Ziegler, who ran a boardinghouse here. The boardinghouse operation continued until the 1980s, when it was converted to apartments.

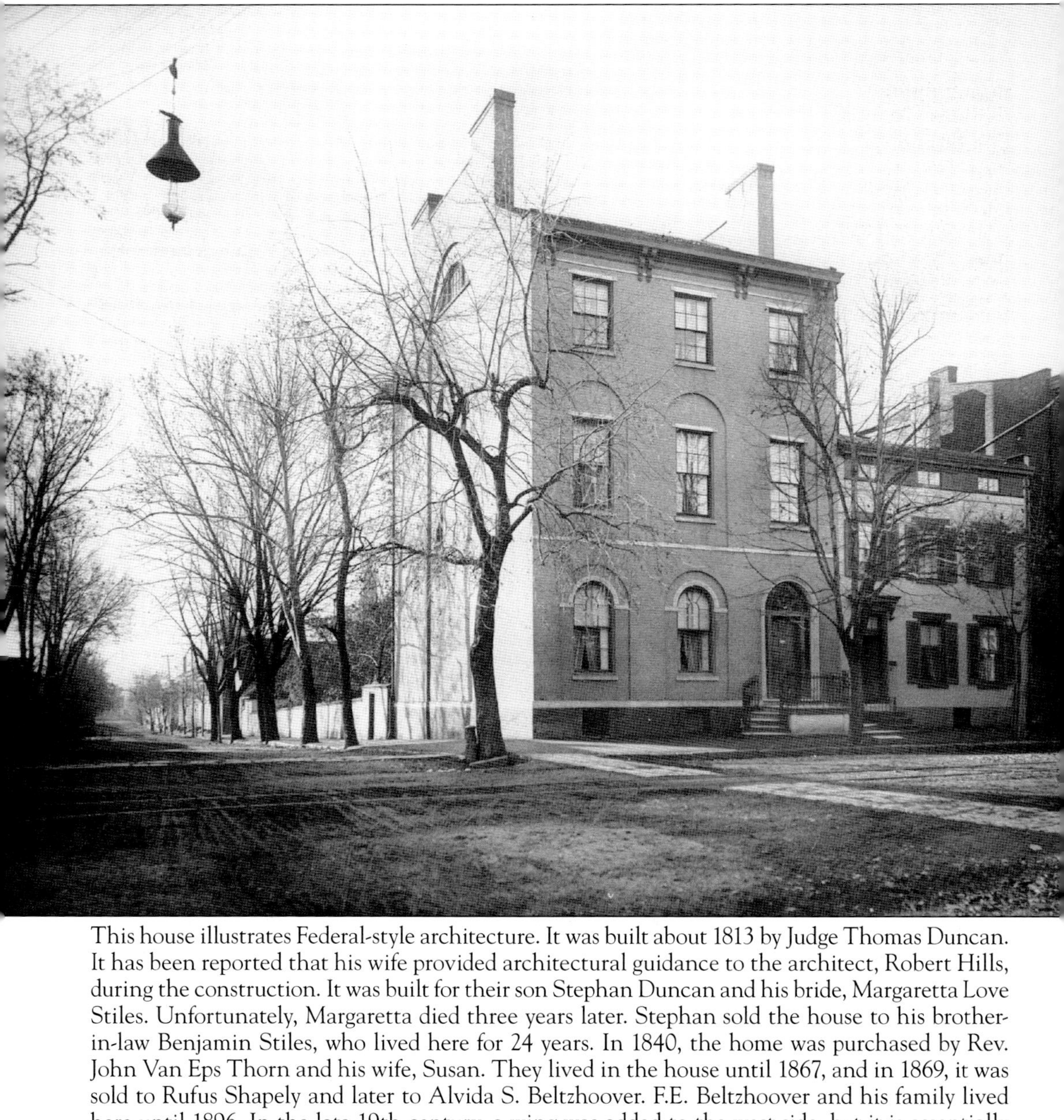

This house illustrates Federal-style architecture. It was built about 1813 by Judge Thomas Duncan. It has been reported that his wife provided architectural guidance to the architect, Robert Hills, during the construction. It was built for their son Stephan Duncan and his bride, Margaretta Love Stiles. Unfortunately, Margaretta died three years later. Stephan sold the house to his brother-in-law Benjamin Stiles, who lived here for 24 years. In 1840, the home was purchased by Rev. John Van Eps Thorn and his wife, Susan. They lived in the house until 1867, and in 1869, it was sold to Rufus Shapely and later to Alvida S. Beltzhoover. F.E. Beltzhoover and his family lived here until 1896. In the late 19th century, a wing was added to the west side, but it is essentially a separate structure. Edward Biddle Jr. owned the house for about 20 years but did not live there. In 1919, John Vovakis, owner of the Sugar Bowl Candy Company, purchased the house, and his family lived there until about 1931.

This cottage at 22 North East Street was built in 1857 by Capt. Thomas Dwen, who had just returned from Brazil where he was constructing railroads. It is a one-and-half-story brick building in the Gothic Victorian style. The first floor has 14-foot ceilings. Captain Dwen was killed in the Battle of South Mountain in Maryland during the Civil War in 1862.

This house at 119 East High Street was built by William Lyon in 1780. He was the son-in-law of Gen. John Armstrong. The house was passed to George Armstrong Lyon, William's son. George was instrumental in the creation of the Second Presbyterian Church in 1832. George died in 1855, and the house was sold to the William Barnitz family. This family still owned the house in 1897.

Molly Pitcher (Mary Hays McCauly) is the heroine of Carlisle. She came from New Jersey to Carlisle to work for Dr. William Irvine and married John Hays on July 24, 1769, in Carlisle. During the Revolutionary War, she served as a cook and nurse and frequently brought pitchers of water to the fighting men. In 1778, at the Battle of Monmouth in New Jersey, legend says she took over the firing of a cannon when her husband was injured. Her home at the southeast corner of Bedford and North Streets is seen above with the logs exposed. At left is her gravesite in the Old Graveyard.

This house at 133 South Hanover Street was owned by James and Janet Ramsey during the Revolutionary War. Janet saved British prisoners Major Andre and Lieutenant Despard from an angry mob in 1776. In the 1870s, Richard and Milton Owen, who were marble carvers, lived in the house. By the 1900s, the Zinn family owned the house, and farm implements were sold here, as seen on the sign.

This house at 28 South Pitt Street was built by the Noble family. In the late 1800s, James Noble and his sons owned the property. Joseph Noble, grandson of James, later owned the property but spent most of his time living elsewhere, including 30 years in Hong Kong. When he died in 1949, the house was sold to George Tallman Ritter, who lived there until the late 1970s.

This building at the southwest corner of South Hanover and West Pomfret Streets was built by Jacob Musselman prior to 1798. He did not live in the house but rented it to Charles Steinecke. The kitchen addition on the back of the building was constructed after 1798.

An inscription in the chinking of this log house at 47 Mulberry Alley reads, "Built 1759 Repaired 1937." According to county records, the first owner was John Reed, who lived there until his death in 1782. The next owners were Joseph Sabolle, John Delaney, and Andrew Hood. Hood died in 1843, and Peter Spahr purchased the building. He was a successful brick manufacturer.

The two lots to the right of the Wellington Hotel were the site of two elegant Colonial houses, as seen at right behind the two trees. The house on the left was the Hepburn House, which had an outstanding Greek Revival entrance. In 1900, these two houses were razed so John S. Low could build his home at 25 East High Street. John Low and his father were liquor dealers. The photograph below was taken in the 1920s. John Low lived here until his death in 1927. In 1928, the house was sold to the Moose Lodge No. 761, which continues at this location today.

This house at 123 South West Street was built around 1880 by George F. Whistler, a tobacco merchant. He died in 1926, but his wife, Mary, and their two children, Edward and Mary, continued to live here. Edward was also a tobacco merchant. He and his wife moved to 243 West Louther Street, and his sister, Mary, continued to live here until 1956. The house was sold in 1968.

The house on the southeast corner of West and Pomfret Streets was built by Anthony Fishburn in the late 1880s. After his death, his wife, Salome, and daughter Louisa lived here until Salome died in 1908. Louisa continued to live here with companions who took care of her until her death in 1938.

Five

HOTELS AND TAVERNS

This house at 137 East High Street was built before 1773 by James Pollock. It was a tavern known as the Sign of the Turk. The property changed owners many times in the early 1800s, and the name was changed to the Sign of the Indian King. One of the owners, James Davis, hosted candlelight balls with traveling dancing masters. The building still stands and is a residence.

The property at 100 North Hanover Street began in 1782 as a tavern named the Sign of the Black Bear. It was a two-story stone building and had two kitchens, a finished shop, and a stone stable. The building was "Victorianized" and renamed the Pennsylvania Inn and later the Pennsylvania House in the mid-1800s, as seen above. From the 1920s through the 1940s, various businesses occupied the property. In 1953, the building was razed, and Carlisle Food Market erected the building seen below and moved to this location. In 1972, it was bought by Giant Food Store. This location closed in 1980.

By 1850, the Cumberland and Perry Inn stood at 164 North Hanover Street. In 1867, the inn was renamed the Thudium House, as seen above, and continued to operate as a hotel and restaurant. This was the location where the Landisburg Stagecoach started its route. In 1927, the Thudium House was torn down, and the first Montgomery Ward in Carlisle was built in its place. It remained here until 1935, when it moved across the street. From 1936 to 1957, the Myers Furniture was at this location. In 1959, Miller's Furniture, seen below, was located at this address and continued here until 1970. Andrews Furniture took over the building in 1972. Presently, the Carlisle Antique Mall is located here.

This building began as a tavern known as the Cross Keys. It was built in the early 1790s by Matthew Allison. Robert Taylor rented the property from David White and opened the tavern in 1806. In 1814, he purchased the property and kept the tavern until 1822, when it was sold by the sheriff. The building has since been a dwelling and still stands today at 176 East Pomfret Street.

This stone building at 131 North East Street was constructed in 1803 by Charles McManus, a tavern keeper who operated the Eagle and the Harp. He also had a distillery, according to advertisements published when he sold the property. McManus died in 1817. This building eventually became a family residence and has recently been restored.

The large brick building at right was constructed by silversmith George Hendel in 1815. It was used as a tavern known as the Sign of General Washington. In the 1820s, the building was converted into two town houses. Judge Bannister Gibson, who served as chief justice of the Pennsylvania Supreme Court, lived on the right side from 1820 until his death in 1853. The building was converted into L.T. Greenfield's Dry Goods Store, with the store entrance on the left. From 1877 to 1883, the store was used by John Haas, a tailor of military and civilian clothing. From the 1920s to the 1940s, 18 East High Street was the location of W.W. Herr and Company Confectioners. In the late 1940s, J.C. Wetzel and Sons Wholesale Confectioners purchased the building (below), and remained there until 1968.

A two-story stone tavern known as the Sign of the Golden Lamb was originally on this corner at 2 East High Street. In 1835, Jacob Zug purchased the property. Between 1856 and 1859, he demolished the tavern and erected a three-story brick building with storefronts. Zug rented the property to various businesses, including Clyde L. Lochman's photography gallery on the second floor, seen here. On his death in 1877, Zug's heirs continued to rent the property. In 1907, Joshua P. Bixler bought the property for the family's hardware store, originally established in 1846 by Henry Saxton and Joshua Bixler. When Saxton died in 1882, his share was bought by the Bixler family. H.T. Herman Shoe Store shared the first floor until 1920, when Bixler took over the entire first floor. The Bixlers closed the business in 1980. Cumberland County purchased the building in 1984, and it eventually became an annex to the courthouse.

In 1802, this was the site of a tavern called the Sign of President Jefferson, a two-story stone building at 17–23 East High Street. The name and owners changed many times through the years until Robert Cornman purchased it in 1843 and called it the Cornman House. Around 1860, Cornman razed the building and erected the first four-story brick structure in Carlisle (above). This would become the Wellington Hotel in the 1890s. A.W. Bentz, the owner in 1869, remodeled the building and added the decorative iron balcony seen below. Rooms were $2 and $2.50 per day, and the hotel provided free transportation to the train station. It closed around 1950.

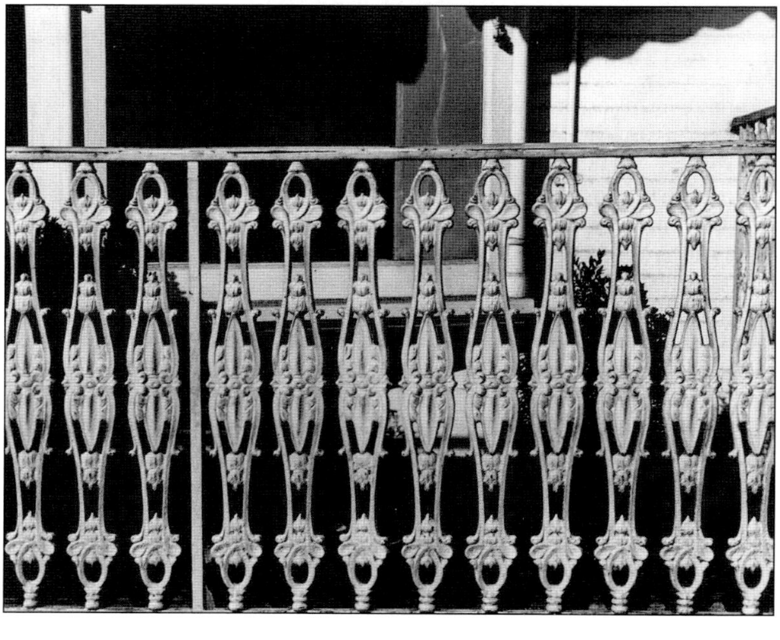

This building at 1 East High Street was originally a two-story stone structure. It first housed a pre-Revolutionary tavern called the Sign of Dickinson College. A third floor was added as well as three storefronts. Later, the front facade was covered with brick. This 1910 photograph shows H.A. Minium's Music House at left. The company sold Moller organs and Victor record players and was located here from about 1904 to 1914. On the second floor was the office of Dr. Curtis Basehoar, a longtime Carlisle dentist, who practiced here from 1904 to 1935. The Singer Sewing Machine Company is at center. On the far right was John E. Sipe's pharmacy, whose business started about 1875 and continued until 1935 when he died. In 1961, the second and third floors became the Irvine Apartments.

The Strohm Building, seen at right, was constructed around 1900. The Strohm Shoe Store was on the first floor, and the upper floors were apartments. In 1919, it was converted to the Hotel Carlisle. The building on the left was replaced with an addition to the hotel. There were 80 rooms and a restaurant. Fifty-four rooms had private baths, and rates started at $2 per day. In 1925, it became the Molly Pitcher Hotel, seen below. The building is located at 11–15 South Hanover Street. In 2007, the building was converted to senior apartments.

This property at 2 South Hanover Street was built in the 18th century as a tavern, which housed George Washington's officers in October 1794 when they were traveling to the Whiskey Rebellion in western Pennsylvania. Among those officers were John Knox, secretary of war, and Alexander Hamilton, secretary of the treasury. It was a two-story stone building and had many tavern keepers through the years. It also had many different names, including Sign of the Sorrel Horse, Sign of the Golden Swan, The Carlisle and Dickinson Inn, and The Green Tree. By the 1840s, it was operating under the name Franklin House. The stone building at right was once part of the tavern and later became the town's post office. The brick building on the left was Kronenberg's Clothing. Samuel Kronenberg, a Confederate veteran, moved to Carlisle and established the clothing store in 1866.

This house on the corner of East Louther and North East Streets was built in the 1760s. At first, it was a tavern with a brewhouse on the property, which consisted of two lots owned by John and Jacob Crever. The tavern keepers in the early 1800s included Philip Lauffman, James Craighead, and Conrad Gross, in addition to Jacob Crever. In the 1830s, William and Mary Alexander purchased the house and made it their family home. Their two sons, William and Samuel, and their three daughters, Jane Mary, Anna, and Laura, lived here with their parents. The family continued to own the house until 1930, when the last living daughter, Laura Alexander, died. She gave the house to her neighbor William S. Egulf Jr. It was later restored by Nancy George in the 1980s, but the brewhouse was beyond repair, so it was demolished.

The Farmers and Drovers Hotel, seen above at 205 South Hanover Street, was built by Samuel Alexander about 1840. It was called by that name because the drovers kept their livestock across the street. In 1860, William Hoaker was the innkeeper. On the 1872 atlas, the owner was N.W. Woods. By 1887, it was owned by George H. Miller and was called the Miller House, seen below. In the early 1900s, it again became known as the Farmers and Drovers Hotel and continued to operate into the 1920s. This building was demolished, and a new one was erected here that today houses Fay's Country Kitchen restaurant.

This stone tavern, the Sign of the Black Bear, was built in the late 1700s at East Louther and Hanover Streets. In the mid-1800s, it became the Pennsylvania Hotel and later the Pennsylvania House. It operated until about 1920, after which it was demolished, and the Pennsylvania Garage was built in its place. Today, the Sadler Medical Building is here.

This property at 101 East High Street was the Garber House in the late 1890s. By the 1900s, it was known as the Cumberland Hotel with William Kline as the proprietor. It was located across from the county jail. From the 1930s through today, the building has been used as apartments, with a retail business occasionally on the first floor.

The property at the southwest corner of High and Pitt Streets began as a tavern that was visited by Dr. Benjamin Rush in 1784. The tavern was replaced by another building known as the Carlisle Hotel. Later, the Carlisle Hotel became the Mansion House. After 1872, the train stopped at the depot next to the Mansion House, making the hotel very convenient for travelers. This continued until a new train station was built across the street in 1891. By 1924, the hotel was renamed the Hotel Argonne, which continued until 1940, when the name was changed to the James Wilson Hotel, as seen here. In 1986, it was no longer a hotel, but was renovated to provide housing for homeless and potentially homeless individuals. It still provides this function today, and is known as Safe Harbor Bridge Housing.

This structure on North Pitt Street was probably built in the early 1900s. It is seen here during an Old Home Week celebration. It was next to the Cumberland Valley train station and provided rooms and a restaurant until sometime in the 1920s. By the late 1930s, the first floor was the St. Charles Café, and the other floors were apartments. The Café Bruges is now on the first floor.

This stone tavern at 200 East High Street was built in the early 1800s as the Sign of Commodore Perry. In the latter part of the 1800s, it became the Letort House. Around 1900, the name changed to Letort Springs Hotel and later just Letort Hotel. Unfortunately, the building was demolished and a service station took it place. The service station is now abandoned.

This stone tavern was built in the late 1700s at East Louther and North Bedford Streets and was known as the Sign of the Flag. It was owned by Capt. Thomas McMurray from 1778 to 1839. His estate was given to his daughter Susannah Higgs. She ran a school in the building. In this photograph, it was a store; today, it is a residence.

This building on Pomfret Street was a tavern known as the Sign of the Ship in the late 1790s. It was built by Jacob Wiser, who was the first tavern keeper. John Moser, a shoemaker, was also a tavern keeper in the early 1800s. After years as a tavern, the building became a residence until 1964, when the Fabric Center opened. It still operates here today.

Six

TRANSPORTATION

In the early 1900s, Carlisle had a city bus. Peter Cook drove his horse-drawn carriage around town providing transportation. It is uncertain how long Cook offered the service, but died in 1912. Whether others also offered the service is not known. At least Peter Cook's ingenuity was recorded for history with this photograph.

The Cumberland Valley Railroad (CVRR) began in 1837. The tracks went straight through the middle of town on High Street. The track was sometimes elevated, as seen above at the intersection of East High and East Streets. In 1848, the first sleeping car in the world was used on the CVRR. The car was named *Chambersburg* and had three sleeping compartments and a washroom. With increased automobile use, the railroad began to lose dominance. The last passenger train rolled through Carlisle on High Street on October 16, 1936 (below). The tracks were removed from High Street to make a wider road for automobiles. The trains were routed off the main thoroughfare north of High Street and continued to service Carlisle.

Although the train started running in 1837, the first depot was not constructed until 1862 on the south side of High Street next to the Mansion House. The photograph at right shows the depot on the far right with a train in front. In 1872, CVRR purchased land adjacent to the depot and in 1875 built a new baggage room and ladies' waiting room. A new station was constructed across the street on the northwest corner of High and Pitt Streets in 1891. It was a one-story brownstone building with a slate roof and large windows, as seen below. When the trains stopped running through downtown in 1936, the station was no longer needed and was sold to Gulf Oil. The company demolished the train station and built a service station.

The Cumberland Valley Electric Passenger Railway began operation in 1895. Separate tracks for trolleys were laid on West, High, and Hanover Streets. The trolley system was established to serve the town and recreational areas and other towns not served by trains. The photograph above shows the trolley in front of the Market House. In 1896, the North Hanover Line was extended to the Carlisle Indian School. Soon after, a line to Cave Hill was established. The company created a park and pavilion there to increase ridership. Lines were also established to parks in Boiling Springs and Mount Holly. The photograph below shows the trolley waiting at the square in the 1920s. The last route established was to Newville. In 1930, the trolleys ceased to operate.

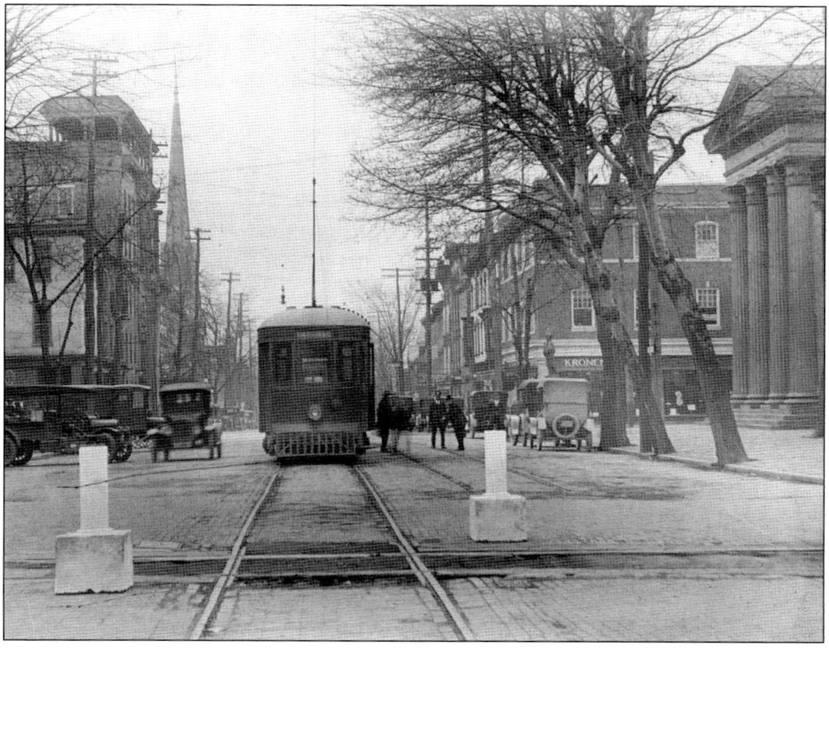

Seven

SIGNIFICANT EVENTS

Carlisle hosted a visit from Gen. Dwight D. Eisenhower on May 21, 1947. General Eisenhower came to give praise to the Army Information Center, which was one of six Army schools established in Carlisle from 1946 to 1947. He presented diplomas to 159 officers and 69 enlisted soldiers at the center. Carlisle honored Eisenhower with a parade. He is seen here riding in Leslie Bentley's yellow Buick convertible.

Carlisle organized the Peace Week Celebration for July 2–4, 1919. The celebration took place in Carlisle and in other Cumberland County communities. On July 3, Carlisle held a huge parade in honor of World War I heroes. The photograph above shows one of the military units marching in front of the courthouse. On July 4, there was a grand historical pageant, which depicted 200 years of Cumberland County history and demonstrated the spirit of freedom and democracy. The photograph below shows a military formation with Revolutionary troops performing in the pageant. The finale of the celebration was a fireworks display.

When Jim Thorpe and Louis Tewanima returned home from the 1912 Olympics in Stockholm, Sweden, Carlisle gave them a homecoming victory parade, pictured above. Thorpe had won gold medals in both the pentathlon and decathlon events. Tewanima won the silver medal in the 10,000 meters and finished 16th in the marathon. Thorpe and Tewanima had attended the Carlisle Indian School, where they had excelled in sports. One year later, Carlisle celebrated the wedding of Thorpe and Iva Miller on October 15, 1913, at St. Patrick Church. The photograph below shows the large wedding party.

Cumberland Fire Company was planning its centennial celebration when some newspapers and local citizens thought to combine it with an Old Home Week celebration. It was planned for the week of August 22–28, 1909. A total of $1,700 was collected for decorations, which included four lighted arches at the square, one over each street. Each arch represented a different fire company. Seen above is the arch over North Hanover Street for the Union Fire Company, which was founded in 1789. Invitations were sent to former residents all over the country, and 10,000 people came to join the celebration. One of the high points of the week was the Firemen's Parade, seen below. The parade had 70 guest fire companies participating plus bands and mounted groups.

Carlisle celebrated its sesquicentennial on October 23 and 24, 1901. The town had a large celebration with lots of decorations. The town square had anniversary arches constructed over both Hanover and High Streets, which were lighted at night. The photograph above shows the crowds under the arches. The celebration included two huge parades, one each day. Below is a Conestoga wagon from 1840 that participated in one of the parades. Another participant was the *Pioneer*, an 1851 locomotive from the Cumberland Valley Railroad that is now in the Smithsonian. In addition, the celebration included concerts and a special exhibit, Mother Cumberland, at the Hamilton Library.

In June 1863, the Civil War came to Carlisle. On June 27, Confederate troops led by Gen. Albert Jenkins captured the town. Gen. Richard Ewell arrived later in the day, and they located their headquarters at the Carlisle Barracks. When the Confederate troops moved toward Harrisburg, Union troops occupied the town. However, on July 1, 1863, Confederate troops led by Gen. Fitzhugh Lee and Gen. J.E.B. Stuart fired on Carlisle in an attempt to recapture the town. The photograph at left shows damage from the shelling on one of the courthouse pillars, while the photograph below shows damage to one of the window sills of the courthouse. The shelling only stopped when the Confederate troops received orders to march to Gettysburg.

About the Cumberland County Historical Society

Originally founded in 1874, the Cumberland County Historical Society is a tremendous regional resource with archival sources documenting county history dating to the 18th century. Its mission is to promote Cumberland County history by demonstrating how history, storytelling, material culture, and preservation can promote social well-being as well as service and citizen engagement through local resources. The archival library contains an extensive collection of original documents and manuscripts as well as over 40,000 published volumes. The photography collection contains over five million historical images. The museum collection contains approximately 10,800 individual artifacts. The society's community outreach programs provide events and educational programs for all ages. Also, the society regularly publishes books and journals. The Cumberland County Historical Society was designated the official historical society for the county by the Cumberland County commissioners in 1987. For more information, visit www.historicalsociety.com.